LIVING IN THE

THE VICTORIANS

GREG THIE

Series editor: Haydn Middleton

Illustrated by Sharon Pallent

SIMON & SCHUSTER
EDUCATION

INTRODUCTION

This book is part of a series on British history. It presents absorbing material on the Victorians, and aims to show the reader that all history is based on *evidence*.

The written sources have been chosen for their vividness and accessibility. In some cases the extracts have been modified to make them simpler for the young reader. All the written evidence is printed in italics throughout the book to distinguish it from the narrative.

The pictorial sources are intended to stimulate close observation and interest. There are follow-up exercises on each double-page spread to encourage the reader to think about the evidence and to develop the important skills of observation, deduction and imaginative reconstruction.

Each book in the series contains double-page spreads on the following topics: Growing Up, Homes, Food and Drink, Clothes and Entertainments. These spreads are identified by recurring symbols on the pages and in the contents list below. Readers who are doing a project on, for example, Growing Up Through the Ages, can find lots of material by looking at the relevant pages in all the books in the series. Finally, in the section on 'HOW TO BE A HISTORIAN', on page 48, there are suggestions for more investigative project work.

CONTENTS

In this book, you will find out a lot about how people lived in Victorian times. But as you read, keep on asking yourself 'How does the writer know this? How does he know that?'. His information about the Victorians comes from things from those days that are still with us today. They might be paintings, books, buildings, photographs or even advertisements. *All* these things help us to work out how life used to be — and in many ways it was very different from life today! The list below shows you what you can find out about in this book. When you have read the whole book, you should be able to say what things have helped the writer to write *all* the stories in the list.

1 A FARMER'S BOY **4** Work and play on the farm	**4 OUR DEAR NELSON IS KILLED** **10** The Battle of Trafalgar and the death of Lord Nelson
2 AT THE MILL **6** How poor children were sent to work in the cotton mills	**5 AN ENGLISHMAN'S HOME** **12** Victorian homes and houses
3 DOWN THE MINE **8** What it was like to work in a coal mine	

2

6 VICTORIA AND ALBERT 14 The story of Queen Victoria and Prince Albert	**16 AN EVENING OUT 34** Going to the music hall
7 THE MAGICAL MACHINE 16 Travelling on the first trains	**17 IT CANNOT DIE 36** Early cars – and the first road accidents
8 THE ARCH OF GLASS 18 All about the Great Exhibition	**18 BESIDE THE SEASIDE 38** Day trips to the seaside and the first holiday resorts
9 FIGHTING JOHNNY RUSS 20 The Crimean War and the Charge of the Light Brigade	**19 THIS WONDERFUL PLACE 40** What happened to people who went abroad to live
10 LOTS OF 'TATURS 22 What rich and poor people ate	**20 THE BRITISH IN INDIA 42** What life was like for British people in India
11 DOCTORS AND NURSES 24 Improvements in medicine and nursing	**21 HOW TO BE AN EXPLORER 44** The men and women who travelled to unknown lands – and what they found there
12 IN FASHION 26 The clothes rich and poor people wore	**22 THE NEW CENTURY 46** People's hopes and fears about the Twentieth Century
13 CHILDREN IN PRISON 28 How Elizabeth Fry tried to make prisons better	**23 HOW TO BE A HISTORIAN 48** How to make your own history book
14 OFF TO SCHOOL 30 All about Victorian schools	
15 AN EVENING IN 32 Some Victorian games and pastimes	

Acknowledgements

The author and publishers are grateful to the following for permission to reproduce photographs:
Reproduced by Gracious Permission of Her Majesty the Queen 20(2); BBC Hulton Picture Library 3(2,3), 7(1), 9(2), 11(3), 15(2), 16(1), 17(1); Beccles and District Museum 6(1); British Library 3(1); The Illustrated London News Picture Library 7(2), 9(1), 19(1); Jarrold Colour Publications 5(1); The Mansell Collection 6(2,3), cover/8(1), 12(1), 17(2), 21(2); Mary Evans Picture Library 1(4), 18(2), 22(1,2,3); Oxfordshire County Libraries 14(2); Victoria and Albert Museum 20(3); Wellcome Institute Library, London 5(3), 11(1,2).

© Greg Thie 1985   All rights reserved.   First published 1985 Reprinted 1987, 1991, 1992   Printed in Hong Kong

Published by Simon & Schuster Education, Campus 400, Maylands Avenue, Hemel Hempstead HP2 7EZ

1 A FARMER'S BOY

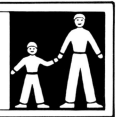

Picture 1 At the start of the nineteenth century almost all the work on the farm was done by men and horses.

William Howitt was born in 1792. He had six brothers. They all lived in a big farmhouse in Derbyshire. At that time most people lived on farms and in small villages, rather than in big towns and cities.

Children had to start work when they were very young. They did all sorts of jobs on the farm. William enjoyed his work. Later, he wrote about some of the things he did:

I remember getting up of a winter moonlight morning at about four o'clock and going off to look at my mole traps in distant fields. . . My days were joyfully spent driving the plough. I helped to hack up frozen turnips for the sheep and cattle. I helped to cut the hay. I filled the racks and cribs with straw for horses and cows. Early in spring, about March, I used to be up in the still bitter frosty mornings to look after the sheep and their lambs.

Picture 1 shows the kind of plough William might have helped to drive. Later on in the year his jobs were:

. . . weeding corn, driving the plough and helping to hoe crops. . . Then came the season for mowing, mushroom gathering, nutting in the woods, collecting acorns for the pigs by the bucketful as they pattered down on a windy day from the trees; threshing; taking in cornstacks, and killing rats and mice, collecting hen, duck, geese and guinea-fowl eggs.

Picture 2

You can see some men *mowing* (cutting grass) in Picture 2. Look at the long knives, or *scythes*, they are using. Picture 3 shows two tools that William did not mention, although he probably used them.

William and the other village boys sometimes got into trouble. One day they went *poaching* for pheasants. But William got caught in a *mantrap* like the one in Picture 4. Then a gamekeeper came and arrested the boys. William was very worried about what would happen to them:

We were to appear in court as poachers — to be punished — perhaps to be hanged!

The boys were lucky. The judge knew their parents, and he let them off — this time.

Picture 3 When William used a dibble and bird-scarer like the ones you can see in this picture, he might have sung rhymes like these:

a dibble

Four seeds in a hole,
One for the rook and
One for the crow.
One to rot, one to grow.

a bird-scarer
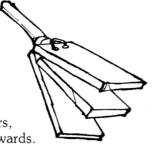

Jackdaws and crows,
Take care of your toes,
For here come my clappers,
To knock you down backwards.

Picture 4 If they were caught, poachers faced being sent to prison for many years, or *transported* (sent away to another country to do hard and heavy work) for life!

✯ ✯ ✯ TO DO ✯ ✯ ✯

1. Draw four columns, headed Winter, Spring, Summer and Autumn. Under each heading list the jobs William did in that season of the year.

2. Look at Picture 3. **a)** What do you think a *dibble* was used for? (The rhyme may help you) **b)** Why do you think the bird-scarer was needed?

3. Pretend you are one of William's friends. Write about what happened on the night you all went poaching. How did you feel when you heard the gamekeeper coming?

2 AT THE MILL

Picture 1

Look at Picture 1. It shows an old mill. Can you see the stream near the building? This drove a big water-wheel which was used to power the machinery inside the mill.

Many children worked in the cotton mills. One of them was called Robert Blincoe. Here is his story.

Robert was an orphan. His parents had died when he was very young. He lived in a big house with many other orphans. When they were seven years old the children were sent to work in the mills. Robert describes what happened:

We were taken in carts. As we got near the mill, the villagers spoke to us. I heard them say 'Poor little things. They don't know that they are now slaves'. At the mill we went into a smelly, oily room. We sat on wooden benches. We had porridge to eat. It was blue. We also had black bread. It was so soft that it stuck to my teeth. I could hardly swallow it. A bell rang. We were taken upstairs. We slept two in each tiny bed. I cried myself to sleep.

At the mill the orphans were called *apprentices*. They were supposed to be learning the job. Picture 2 shows some apprentices in a cotton mill, and the sorts of machines they worked with. Some of the mill-owners were cruel men. They treated the apprentices very harshly. Robert was often punished. Years later he wrote:

Once I had two heavy weights screwed behind my ears. I still have the scars. Another time I was tied to a beam and hung over the moving machinery. Sometimes I was hit with a strap or a stick.

You might think Robert had done something very bad to be punished like this. But apprentices could be punished for all sorts of things. Here are a few of them:

- *looking out of the window*
- *riding on each others' backs*
- *telling lies*
- *throwing tea at each other*

Some apprentices ran away because they could not stand life at the mill. The owners tried to get them back. They put advertisements in the newspapers, like the one in Picture 3.

Robert Blincoe was lucky. After a while he moved to another mill, where he had a kind master. This was the mill you can see in Picture 1.

Picture 3

RUN AWAY

from Cromford Cotton Mills in the county of Derby; John Flint. He has red hair and has a mole on his face. Whoever will give information to Mr RICHARD ARKWRIGHT of Cromford – the person that employs the above apprentice, shall be handsomely rewarded for their trouble.

Picture 2 Life was hard for most apprentices. They had to work long hours. Sometimes their masters were cruel men, who punished them harshly. The work was dangerous, too, because there were no safety-guards on the machines.

☆☆☆ TO DO ☆☆☆

1. Make a list of all the things you can see happening in Picture 2. Do you think this mill-owner was a cruel or a kind man?

2. Imagine you have found John Flint, the runaway apprentice (see Picture 3). Write down what he tells you about his life at the mill and why he ran away. What will you do next? Will you help him hide? Or will you send him back to his master and claim the reward?

3 DOWN THE MINE

Picture 1 Colliers being lowered down a mine. What possible dangers can you see in the picture?

Near the farm in Derbyshire where William Howitt lived (see page 4) was a coal mine. Men, women and children worked there, deep underground.

One night William was taken to see the colliers (coal miners) at work:

As I rode over the hill I suddenly saw strange lights in front of me in every direction. I could also hear sad sounds like groans and sighs. My friend. . . told me that the fires were burning by the coal pits. The sounds I heard were the sounds of machinery which pulled up the coal and drained the pits of water.

When William got closer he could see some colliers getting ready to go down into the mine. The holes were over 200 metres deep. William

. . . shuddered to see the colliers go near the holes, even more when they sit on a single chain and hook it to the end of a huge rope. This hangs over the pit and they are lowered to the bottom.

Picture 1 shows two colliers being lowered into a mine.

William at last plucked up courage to go down a pit.

I was dressed in a flannel frock lent to me by a pit boy. I wore a round crowned hat without a brim. It was well stuffed with hay.

William sat on a miner's knee and they were lowered down into the mine.

. . . around us gushed water from the bricks which lined the side of the pit. As I looked up the daylight looked like a small star above me. Then I heard human voices sounding deeply like echoes. To my delight we soon felt solid ground beneath us. What a wild, gloomy and strange scene. A black cave was in front of me. We went on a good way.

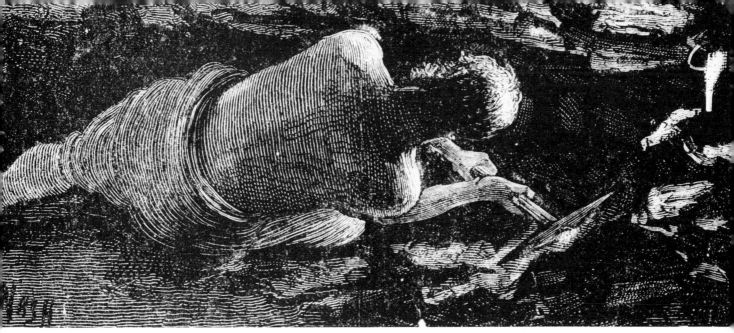

Picture 2

Suddenly there were the lights that the colliers use while they work. Here the poor fellows sit on the ground at the coalface... They use their sharp picks to dig the bottom of the coalface.

Sometimes the tunnels were so small the miners had to work lying down, like the man in Picture 2. William went on:

Then comes the hammer man with his hammer. He knocks down a mass of coal. They load it onto the truck. A little pony draws it along a little railway to the pit mouth. (See Picture 3.)

Mining was a very hard job. It could be dangerous, too:

As the poor miners clear away the coal they prop the roof up with pieces of wood. This is to stop the earth above them falling in. Sometimes it does do this and they are crushed to death or left alive to starve before their friends can dig them out.

Picture 3 In many pits ponies were used to haul the loads of coal. They spent almost all their lives in darkness, deep underground.

✶ ✶ ✶ TO DO ✶ ✶ ✶

1. What were the 'strange lights' that William saw? What made the 'sad sounds'? How did the colliers get down into the pit?

2. Why do you think the miners wore hats stuffed with hay?

3. Why was mining such a dangerous job? Read William's descriptions again and look at the pictures. List as many dangers as you can.

4 'OUR DEAR NELSON IS KILLED'

Dear Father,

This letter comes to tell you that I am alive and well — except for three fingers — but that's not much. It might have been my head!

The French and Spaniards fought us pretty hard. Three of our group were killed. Four were injured. To tell the truth, when the battle started I wished I was back at Warnborough with my plough again... How my fingers got knocked overboard I don't know — but they are off!

We have captured many ships but the wind is so rough that we can't get them back to port. Instead, we are busy smashing 'em and blowing 'em up.

Our dear Admiral Nelson is killed. I never saw him. I am both sorry and glad about this. The men who have seen him have done nothing but cry ever since he was killed.

I am still in my ship the Royal Sovereign. The Admiral, Lord Collingwood, has left for a while. I saw his tears with my own eyes when the boatmen came to say Nelson was dead. No more at present from your son.

Sam

Sam was a sailor in the British Navy. He had just taken part in the Battle of Trafalgar. The Admiral of the British fleet was Lord Nelson. His ship was called the Victory. You can see what it was like in Picture 1.

Picture 1

Sam did not see what happened to Nelson. But a marine on board the Victory gives us this eye-witness report. He saw a French ship nearby, and

. . . heavy musket fire come from the top of the mast. At 1.15 Nelson was walking with Captain Hardy. He was shot through the shoulder. He fell face down on the deck. Hardy ordered the Admiral to be carried below deck. Nelson covered his face with a handkerchief as he was carried past the crew.

Down below, the ship's doctor tried to help. His name was Dr Beatty. He was there when Nelson died:

Every time an enemy ship surrendered, the crew of the Victory cheered. Nelson was pleased when he was told this. . . His voice got fainter. His hand grew cold. The pulse had gone. He breathed his last at 4.30.

Picture 1   This picture shows what the *Victory* was like above and below decks. Points **1**-**4** show:
1   Lord Nelson's cabin
2   Captain Hardy's cabin
3   Where Nelson was shot
4   Where Nelson died

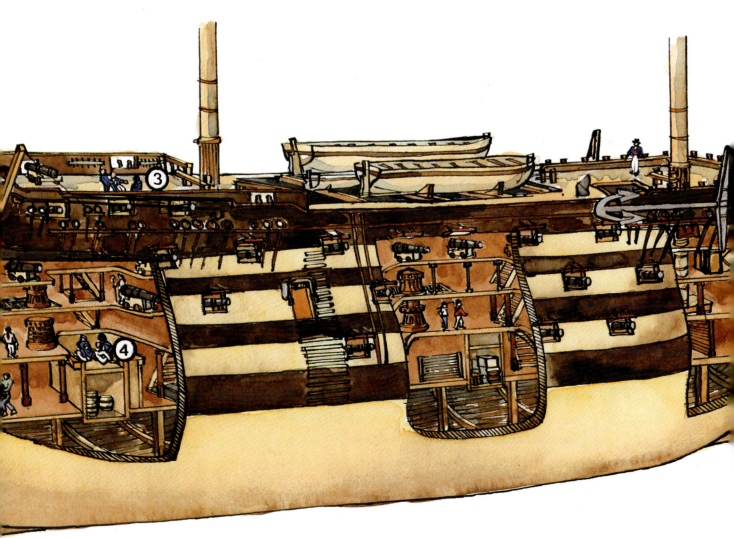

5 AN ENGLISHMAN'S HOME

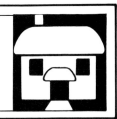

Picture 1 This photograph shows the outside of Harlaxton Hall, Mr Gregory's house, today.

Picture 2 is a plan showing all the rooms on the ground floor. How many are there?

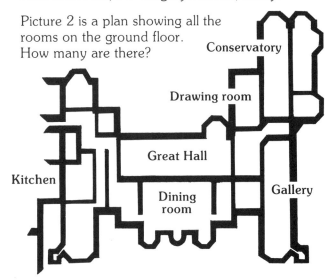

In January 1838 Charles Greville went to visit a country house while it was being built.

Today we went to see the house that Mr Gregory is building. He is now in the middle of his work, all the shell being finished except one wing. Many years ago when he first thought of the idea of building such a house, he began to save money and collect objects from all over Europe for his palace. He says that it is his amusement instead of hunting, shooting or feasting.

You can see the house he visited in Picture 1. The house was started in 1832 and took ten years to build. Picture 2 shows the plan for the ground floor. It was a very grand house. There was hot air heating and even a covered railway that brought coal and wood to the house.

Hundreds of big country houses like Harlaxton Hall were built in Victorian times. At the same time many thousands of other houses were being built, too, all over Britain. These were not at all grand. A Government report said:

A huge number of small houses are built by members of building clubs. They are built back to back. Like a honey comb every particle of space is occupied. Double rows of three houses form courts. Perhaps there is one water pump at one end and a privy (toilet) at the other — used by the people living in the 20 houses.

Picture 3 shows some of these *back-to-back* houses. Another report, by a medical officer, described:

44 houses in two rows. There are 22 cellars. There is a common gutter between the houses. All sorts of rubbish is thrown here. Things rot and poison the air.

The Victorian writer Charles Kingsley visited a town and was horrified to see "*people drinking the water from the sewer, which was full of dead fish, cats and dogs*".

In spite of the dreadful conditions many people worked hard to keep their houses clean. A visitor to a poor area wrote

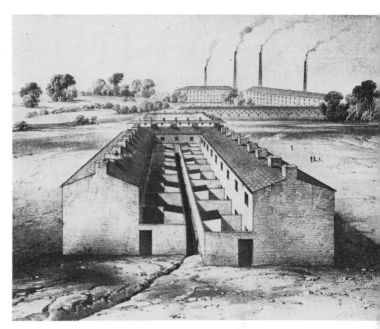

Picture 3   These houses were built for factory workers. How do they compare with the house in Picture 1?

It was sad to see how they washed the floors and steps clean and hung their washed clothes out to dry, only to see them dirtied by soot from the neighbouring furnaces. . . and in spite of all their care their children pale, sickly and drooping.

☆☆☆ TO DO ☆☆☆

1. What can you see at points 1-5 on Picture 1? (Use Picture 2 to help you.)

2. Why do you think the children living in houses like the ones in Picture 3 were 'pale, sickly and drooping'? Make a list of all the reasons you can find.

3. What else can you see in Picture 3? What might this tell you about the people who lived in these houses?

6 VICTORIA AND ALBERT

Queen Victoria ruled Britain from 1837 until her death in 1901. This book is all about the things that happened while she was Queen. That is why it is called THE VICTORIANS.

Victoria was only 18 when she became Queen. This is how she heard the news:

I was woken at 6 o'clock by Mamma. She told me some important people wanted to see me. I got out of bed. I was in my dressing gown. The two men told me that my poor Uncle, the King, had died at 12 minutes past 2 this morning. As a result I am Queen!

Victoria's Coronation was celebrated all over Britain. Picture 1 shows what people did in one Suffolk village.

Victoria's husband was called Albert. He was a German prince. Albert had come

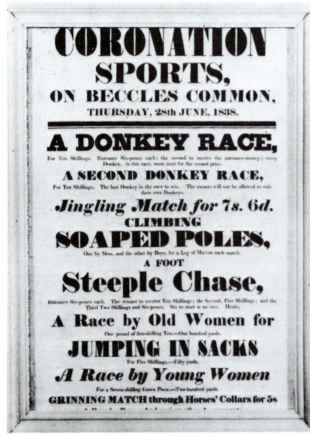

Picture 1 The people of Beccles obviously had fun on Queen Victoria's Coronation Day.

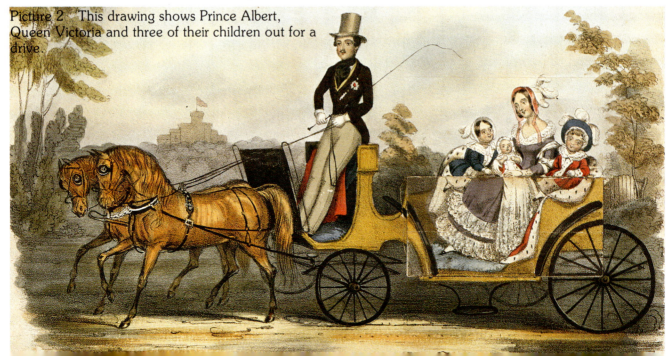

Picture 2 This drawing shows Prince Albert, Queen Victoria and three of their children out for a drive.

to England soon after Victoria had become queen. At first he was not sure if he would like her. People had told him that she was "*very stubborn. That she loves silly manners and shows. She also stays up late and then sleeps for much of the morning.*" But Victoria and Albert did like each other, and they agreed to marry.

At first many people did not like Albert. They thought it was wrong for a British queen to marry a foreigner. Over the years Albert became more popular. This was partly because of his idea for the Great Exhibition, which you can read about on pages 18-19 of this book.

Victoria and Albert had nine children. Albert was a good father. He enjoyed playing with the children (see Picture 2).

In 1861 Albert died of a disease called typhoid. Victoria wrote in her diary "*All alone. Now there is no-one left to call me Victoria.*"

The Queen was very lonely without Albert. She hid herself away for many years. Some people said that she was not doing her job properly. Later she began to appear in public again.

In 1897 Victoria had been Queen for 60 years. Special celebrations were held. Russell Thorndike was a choirboy at St Paul's Cathedral on the day. This is what he wrote in his diary for 22 June 1897:

Arrived in London at 7 am. Went to St Paul's Cathedral. We ate a few sandwiches and had some lemon squash, mixed with tap water. We were worried about the tap water as it seemed to come

Picture 3 After Prince Albert died, Queen Victoria had this special *memorial* built for him. You can still see it in Kensington Gardens, in London.

from the graves in the churchyard. We took our places. Oh! What a sight. All the soldiers were there. The Queen was dressed in black silk with a black bonnet. She looked well and ever so happy. All the people joined in singing 'God Save the Queen'.

Queen Victoria died in 1901. Russell Thorndike had to sing at her funeral, too. He wrote:

It was not until the procession had passed into darkness that I realised Victoria the Great was dead.

7 'THE MAGICAL MACHINE'

Have you ever travelled by train? When Queen Victoria came to the throne in 1837 hardly anyone could have answered 'Yes' to that question.

Railways were still very new and exciting. Picture 1 shows one of the early passenger trains. Picture 2 shows the opening of a new railway line at Swansea. Here is how one lady described her first railway journey to a friend who had never been on a train:

You can't imagine how strange it seemed to be journeying in this way, pulled by the magical machine with the flying white breath. I felt as if no fairy tale was ever half so wonderful as what I saw. I stood up with my bonnet off and drank the air before me. When I closed my eyes the sensation of flying was quite delightful.

One of the railway builders was a famous engineer called George Stephenson. The same lady had a conversation with him.

He had travelled on the Manchester-Liverpool railroad for many miles at the speed of one mile each minute. He told me that he could make his engines travel faster than any bird. He had worked out that the highest speed the human body could stand was 400 miles per hour.

Although it was exciting, railway travel could be uncomfortable. One traveller remembered a journey he took in 1837:

I travelled by train to London in what is now an ordinary goods truck. There was neither roof nor seats. If it rained or the wind was cold the passengers sat on the floor and protected themselves as best they could. This was a third class carriage. The second class carriages were closed in but low and nearly dark with plain wooden seats, while the first class were exactly like the bodies of three stage coaches joined together.

Books were written to tell new passengers how to behave. Here are two things to remember from *Rules for Railway Travelling*:

Picture 1

Picture 2

- On some lines seats are put on the carriage roofs. These should be avoided!
- Be careful not to jump out of the carriage to try to get back a lost hat...

Sometimes the rules were very strict. Here is one from the Manchester to Liverpool railway:

No smoking is allowed in any First Class carriage, even if all the passengers agree. This is because it would annoy passengers on the following journey.

✯✯✯ TO DO ✯✯✯

1. Look at Picture 2. Write down everything you can see happening in the picture. What do you think the spectators are saying?

2. Write down as many differences as you can think of between railway travel in 1837 and railway travel today. (**Clues**: open carriages, seating, steam engines, speed.)

8 THE ARCH OF GLASS

Picture 1 The Crystal Palace in Hyde Park. Work began on 26 September 1850. The building took 250 000 metres of glass, 3300 pillars, 2300 iron girders and 30 miles of gutters! The cost of building it came to £80 000.

In chapter 6 you read about Queen Victoria's husband, Prince Albert. Albert had a wonderful idea. He wanted to hold a great exhibition of all the best things made by the peoples of the world.

The Great Exhibition took place in London in 1851. A huge building was put up in Hyde Park to hold all the exhibits (see Picture 1). It was called the Crystal Palace.

Queen Victoria visited the Crystal Palace while the exhibition was being prepared. Afterwards she wrote in her diary:

April 19th *We went up into the Gallery. The sight of the Exhibition from there — full of all sorts of objects — had the effect of fairy land. The noise was tremendous, at least 12 000 (people) working. The clocks, silver, English ribbons, lace etc are beautiful. We went down and examined the French part, looked also at the Italian, Portuguese, Spanish, and German parts. The Austrian section is quite beautiful. There are porcelain and iron from Berlin and embroideries from Switzerland. Russia is far behind as the ships were frozen in and could not bring the things sooner.*

Before the Exhibition was opened the floors had to be tested. Ranks of soldiers marched over the floorboards to make sure they would bear the weight of all the visitors. It was a good job the floors were strong – six million people visited the Exhibition in the first six months.

Queen Victoria opened the Great Exhibition on 1 May 1851. All kinds of people came to see it (see Picture 2). One man wrote:

At first the Exhibition was crowded with rich people. Now the visitors are the poorer people. They walk or come by train. These visitors know what they want to see. They hurry to the locomotive section or watch the new mill machinery. It is more like a school than a show.

All these visitors needed food and drink. By the end of the Exhibition they had eaten 12 000 cakes; 60 000 loaves of bread; 1 800 000 buns and 2000 pineapples. They drank 1 000 000 bottles of lemonade, soda and ginger beer. Perhaps that explains the success of another new idea at the Exhibition: public toilets. The toilets cost £1600 to build. People had to pay to use them. When this money was added up it came to £1900.

The Great Exhibition took place halfway through the nineteenth century. People were very proud of all the new inventions and beautiful things they had seen. They thought that life would get better and better in the *next* 50 years.

Picture 2   There was something for everyone at the Great Exhibition. People came from all over the country to see it.

✯ ✯ ✯ TO DO ✯ ✯ ✯

1. a) Name six countries that sent things to the Great Exhibition. **b)** Why was Russia 'far behind'? **c)** How long did it take to build the Crystal Palace? How much did it cost? **d)** How were the floorboards tested?

2. Imagine you are writing an entry in your diary for 3 August 1851. Begin 'Went to London by train to visit the Great Exhibition. . .' Then write down everything you saw and did that day. What did you have to eat? What part of your day did you like best?

9 FIGHTING 'JOHNNY RUSS'

Picture 1 The Seige of Sebastopol, in the Crimea.

In 1854 Britain and France were fighting a war against the Russians. It was fought in a part of southern Russia called the Crimea.

Thousands of British soldiers and sailors were sent to fight in the Crimean War. But they were not given enough of the right equipment. When winter came it was bitterly cold (see Picture 1). The men suffered terribly. William Howard Russell was a reporter for *The Times* newspaper. He was sent to find out about the war. This is what he wrote:

Hundreds of men go into the trenches at night with no proper covering and only shoes on their feet. The trenches are two or three feet deep with mud, snow and half-frozen slush. Many men can't get their swollen feet back into their shoes if they take them off. They then have to hop to the camp in snow half a foot deep.

In spite of the bad conditions the troops fought bravely. One officer described how, when the British guns fired, his men "*would all leap out of the trench, wave the Union Jack and cheer like devils*" until the Russians started shooting back.

One sailor wanted to capture something from 'a living Rooshian'.

He saw a big flat-capped, long-coated one hiding in nearby bushes. Like a shot he set off. Johnny Russ (a nick-name for the Russian soldiers) *ran too. In a few seconds the seaman had grabbed the soldier by the neck. He shook him. He took the musket out of his hand. Then he gave him a kick or two on the behind before coming back with the gun.*

One of the most famous battles in the war was the Battle of Balaclava. During this battle a terrible mistake was made. 600 British soldiers were given the wrong orders. They charged against a much bigger Russian army, armed with heavy guns. A soldier called Henry Clifford was watching:

I saw shells bursting. . . and men and horses strewed the ground behind them; yet on they went. . . The tears ran down my face. . . Then the smoke cleared away and I saw hundreds of our poor fellows lying on the ground. Horses without riders galloped back in numbers, and men on foot. At length about 30 horse-men dashed through, and then another larger group came in sight. 200 men were all that returned out of 600 that charged.

Later, this became known as the Charge of the Light Brigade. Picture 2 is a drawing of this famous charge. Despite this disaster, the war dragged on for another two years until finally, in 1856, the British soldiers and sailors returned home.

☆ ☆ ☆ TO DO ☆ ☆ ☆

1. As if you were one of the sailors in Picture 1, write a story about the Crimean War. (**Clues:** conditions in the trenches; the bitter cold; poor equipment; waiting to attack; how you feel about the Russians.)

2. Draw your own picture of the Charge of the Light Brigade, using Henry Clifford's words and Picture 2 to help you.

Picture 2   The Charge of the Light Brigade.

10 LOTS OF 'TATURS'

Have you ever bought food at a market? Do you remember the cries of the stall-holders as they tried to get you to buy their fruit or vegetables or fish?

In Victorian times hundreds of food-sellers walked the streets of the big cities, shouting out what they had to sell. They were called *costermongers*.

All the goods that they sell are cried or hawked. Here are some of the main cries: Ni-ew mackerel, six a shilling; pine-apples one penny the slice; salmon two a penny; penny a bunch turnips; we-ild Hampshire rabbits, two a shilling; cherry ripe two pence a pound; eels, large live eels three pounds for a shilling.

Picture 1 shows some costermongers in the London streets.

The costermongers did not often get a chance to eat any of the food they sold.

They have their breakfast at a coffee stall — a small coffee and two thin slices of bread and butter. For dinner — which on a weekday is hardly ever eaten at home — they buy small dark meat from the cheap butchers. If there isn't time the coster buys a hot fruit pie or meat pie. 'We never eat eel pies' said one coster 'because we know they're often made of dead large eels.' On Sunday the coster enjoys a good dinner at home. This is always a joint or half-shoulder of mutton — and 'lots of good 'taturs'.

Poor people ate very plain food. This is a week's shopping list for a labourer, his wife and their three children:

Picture 1

Five loaves
Seven pints porter (beer)
Forty pounds of potatoes
Five pounds of meat
One pound butter
One pound sugar
Three ounces of tea

Mrs B lived in a well-off part of London. She was married to a shop-keeper. They were not really rich — but they certainly were not poor. People like this could afford much more varied food. Mrs B listed the dinners they ate in one week:

Sunday — Roast beef, potatoes, greens, Yorkshire pudding.
Monday — Hashed beef and potatoes.
Tuesday — Boiled beef and bones, vegetables and spotted dick pudding.
Wednesday — Fish (if cheap), chops and vegetables.
Thursday — Boiled pork, peas pudding, greens.
Friday — Peas soup, remains of pork.
Saturday — Stewed steak with suet dumplings.

Picture 2

Mr B's business did very well, and soon they became rich. They could afford to entertain guests and eat very well. Picture 2 shows the menu for a dinner party Mrs B gave. All this food was eaten by 12 people!

✯✯✯ TO DO ✯✯✯

1. Make a list of six things the costermongers sold.

2. Look at the poor family's shopping list. Do you think they had a healthy diet? Why do you think they ate so many potatoes?

3. Write out a list of all the main meals you ate last week. How does it compare with Mrs B's list?

11 DOCTORS AND NURSES

In those days a patient was like a criminal getting ready to be executed. He counted the days to the time of the operation. On the day he counted the hours. Then he listened for the sound of the surgeon's carriage. He listened for the door bell. He watched the surgeon come in and the feared instruments (knives and saws) appear. Then he gave up his freedom. He was held down and tied up.

This is part of a letter sent to Dr James Simpson. The person who wrote it was describing what it was like to have an operation in the days before *anaesthetics*. (Anaesthetics put patients to sleep during operations so that they feel no pain.) In 1847 Dr Simpson had discovered an anaesthetic called *chloroform*. This grateful patient was writing to thank him.

Picture 1 shows what happened when chloroform was tested for the first time.

Picture 1

Picture 2

At first many people were too frightened to use chloroform. But after Queen Victoria used it to have her babies, chloroform became more popular. The Royal Doctor wrote to Dr Simpson:

Her Majesty was greatly pleased with the effect. I know this will please you. I have no doubt that it will lead to more general use of chloroform.

Chloroform made things much better for patients during operations. But what happened to them afterwards, in hospital?

In the crowded cities, people are more likely to die if they are treated IN a hospital than if they are treated OUT of it.

That was written by a lady called Florence Nightingale (see Picture 2). She worked hard to make life better for sick people in Victorian times.

Florence Nightingale had read about the Crimean War in *The Times* (see pages 20-21). She decided to go to the Crimea and help the wounded soldiers.

After the war Miss Nightingale returned to Britain. She visited some hospitals and was shocked at what she saw. They were dirty and overcrowded, and most of the nurses were untrained. Miss Nightingale was determined to change things.

A writer called Mrs Gaskell knew Florence Nightingale. Here is how she described her to a friend:

She is tall and slight. She has merry eyes and perfect teeth. She has no friend and she wants none. She used to go a great deal among the villagers here. Now she will not as her heart and soul are in her hospital plans.

The first of Miss Nightingale's 'hospital plans' was to improve the training of nurses (see Picture 3). She set up The Nightingale School of Nursing at St Thomas' hospital in London. Miss Nightingale was very strict with her new nurses. After they had been at the school for a while she wrote reports on them. Here are a few of her comments:

Nurse W: *Useful little person.*
Nurse G: *Makings of a nice nurse.*

Picture 3   Florence Nightingale (by now an old lady), with some of her nurses, in 1886.

Willing, good in the ward.
Miss B: *No love of the job — wants amusement.*
Nurse M: *Good — quiet and religious.*
Miss C: *A capital little woman. No education but she seems as good as she can be. No complaints. Keen on work.*

✫✫✫ TO DO ✫✫✫

1. a) Why was chloroform so important? **b)** Who helped chloroform become popular? **c)** What do you think is happening in Picture 1?

2. Make a list of the things that Florence Nightingale looked for in a good nurse. What do you think happened to Nurse B?

3. Why might people be more likely to die in a hospital than out of one? How did Florence Nightingale make things better?

12 IN FASHION

Picture 1

Look at Picture 1. What do you think is happening? This picture is called *Dressing for the Ball in 1857*. It shows a young lady getting dressed. Her maids are helping her put on a *crinoline*. The crinoline was a steel or wire frame which went under ladies' very full dresses.

Although the crinoline was very fashionable it was not at all easy to wear. This is what happened to some ladies who visited a show:

On coming to the turnstile (the only entrance) it was discovered that the ladies could not squeeze through so small a space. The only answer was to open the great gates.

Sometimes crinolines could be quite dangerous:

One accident was caused by a dress being caught by a cab wheel while the lady was crossing the street. Here the victim escaped with a broken leg!

If you look at Picture 1 again you can see some of the lady's underclothes. Well-off ladies wore many layers of underclothes. One young man pretended to be asleep while the ladies were dressing. But he peeped — and this is what he saw:

1 Thick, long-legged long-sleeved combinations. 2 Over them white cotton combinations with frills. 3 Bony grey stays and suspenders. 4 Black woollen stockings. 5 White cotton drawers with buttons and frills. 6 White cotton petticoat with buttons and frills. 7 Short white flannel petticoat. 8 Long petticoat. 9 Pink flannel blouse. 10 High buttoned boots.

Poor people could not afford to dress fashionably or have so many clothes. Look at Picture 2. It shows costermongers like the ones you read about on pages 22-23.

They usually wear a small cloth cap a little on one side. They don't wear hats because of the baskets they usually wear on their heads. They rarely have coats and their waistcoats go up to their throats. The trousers are dark cable cord. They fit tightly to the knee and then swell until they reach the boot which they nearly cover. They all wear silk neckerchiefs – a yellow pattern on a green background is in fashion.

Picture 2
Costermongers

Picture 3

In the country fashions did not change much. People's clothes had to last them a long time. Picture 3 shows the sort of clothes country people wore. This is how a boy called Eli's grandparents dressed:

. . . grandfather wore corduroy trousers and a linen smock frock with a red neck handkerchief and a shaggy top hat on Sundays. 'Granmer' dressed in a full-skirted gown, a woollen shawl and a black coal-scuttle bonnet made of silk.

✫ ✫ ✫ TO DO ✫ ✫ ✫

1. Draw your own picture to show: **a)** a rich lady's clothes; **b)** costermongers' clothes **c)** country people's clothes. Which sort of clothes would you most like to wear? Why?

2. What materials were the Victorian lady's clothes made of? Make a list of all the clothes you are wearing and what they are made of. How do the materials differ? Why do you think this is?

13 CHILDREN IN PRISON

Picture 1

HUNTINGDON COUNTY GAOL

PARTICULARS of a Person convicted of a Crime

Name and Aliases: Dennis Fairey
Age: 9 years
Height: 3ft 9 inches
Hair: Brown
Eyes: Blue
Complexion: Pale
Where born: Ellington, Hunts
Married or single: Single
Trade or occupation: School Boy
Any other distinguishing marks: None

Photograph of Prisoner

Address: Huntingdon
Place and date of conviction: Huntingdon, 19th Dec. 1876
Offence for which convicted: Stealing a loaf of Bread, oranges, apples and Nuts

A lady called Elizabeth Fry and her friend Anna Buxton were inside Newgate Prison in London. They had brought bundles of clean clothes to give to the prisoners. First they went to see the Prison Governor.

The Governor warned Elizabeth to leave her watch in his office. Then he took them into the huge cells. There were 300 women there and 70 children. All these people had to cook, wash, eat and sleep there. They all slept on the floor. They had no mats to make beds. Many were drunk. It was filthy dirty. The smell was disgusting.

The two ladies were shocked by what they saw. But they came back the next day. They especially wanted to help the children. Anna Buxton remembered the visit later

I felt as if we were going into a den of wild animals. I was frightened when we were locked in. We began to teach the prisoners to read.

These visits, and many more like them, eventually led to changes for the better in the prisons. There were fewer prisoners in each cell, and they were given better food. Yet 60 years after Elizabeth Fry first visited Newgate in 1814 one thing at least has not changed: children were still being locked up in prison. Here are some examples from police files:

1872 Julia Orgothorpe: lives in Grantham. Aged 11. Stole a loaf. Sentence – two weeks in prison.
1875 Sam Hayes: lives in Grantham. Aged 12. Stole window locks. Sentence – two weeks hard labour (work) in prison. Nine hits with the birch.

Picture 1 shows the prison sheet for another boy. What crimes had he committed?

The men in Picture 2 are on a *treadwheel*. They had to walk for hours – without getting anywhere. Here is what one boy said:

At 9 we were taken to the weel room. It was like walking up steps and never getting any higher. It was verry hard work. We worked for three hours. Then came dinner. We were on the weel again from 1 to 4. Then we were sent to pick oakum till 8 when we went to bed.

Picture 2 Prisoners on a treadwheel. As well as being a form of punishment, treadwheels were sometimes used to provide power for the prison.

✯✯✯✯✯✯✯✯ TO DO ✯✯✯✯✯✯✯✯

1. a) Why did the prison governor warn Elizabeth Fry to leave her watch? **b)** How many people were in a cell in Newgate? **c)** How was Sam Hayes punished?

2. a) What had Dennis Fairey done? **b)** Why do you think he stole those particular things? **c)** What time of the year was it? Do you think that helps explain his crime?

14 OFF TO SCHOOL

Do you remember William and Robert from the early chapters of this book? What did they do all day? You probably noticed that they did not go to school like you and your friends.

Until around 1870 most poor children started work when they were very young. They did not go to school at all. Some villages had *Dame* schools like the one in Picture 1. There were also charity schools, or *ragged* schools, which were often run by churches.

Children learned the '3 Rs' – Reading, 'Riting and 'Rithmetic. They were also taught how to behave. Here are some rules from one charity school:

1 To come to School at Nine in the Morning and Two in the Afternoon. 2 To attend School with Hands and Face clean. 3 On all occasions to speak the Truth. 4 To avoid all bad Company. 5 Never to use bad Words or Names. 6 To avoid all quarrelling. 7 To be Silent in School.

Things had changed by the end of Queen Victoria's reign. After 1876 an Act of Parliament said that all children had to go to school between the ages of five and ten. In 1891 *elementary* (infant and junior) education was made free for all children. School Boards were set up all over the country to build new schools, like the one in Picture 2.

Flora Thompson went to one of the new schools in the 1880s. She wrote about it in her book *Lark Rise to Candleford*.

School began at 9 but the children set off on their mile and a half walk as as soon as possible after their 7 o'clock breakfast. They carried their flat rush dinner baskets over their shoulders. In cold weather some of them carried two hot potatoes... The one large classroom had several windows. Beyond was a playground enclosed with white painted palings... The girls wore ankle-length frocks and long straight pinafores. The bigger boys in corduroys and hob-nailed boots – the smaller ones in home made sailor suits or petticoats if they were under 7... Reading, writing and arithmetic were the main subjects with a scripture lesson every morning and needlework every afternoon for the girls.

Picture 1

Picture 2 You can still see Victorian school buildings like this in many towns.

Picture 3 Flora Thompson's classroom probably looked like this. Notice how high the windows are – so the children would not look outside instead of doing their lessons.

> ✯ ✯ ✯ **TO DO** ✯ ✯ ✯
>
> **1. a)** What were the '3 Rs'? **b)** Can you think of two reasons why the children carried hot potatoes to school?
>
> **2.** Compare your classroom and school with the Victorian schools shown and described here. Make one list for things that are the same and another for things that are different. (**Clues**: desks, walls, windows, lessons, number of pupils, what they are wearing. . .)

15 AN EVENING IN

How do you spend your free time indoors. Do you watch television or listen to the radio? Perhaps you play records or cassettes, or hire a film on video?

In Victorian times none of these things had been invented. People had to make their own amusements. They might invite friends round for a musical 'at home', like the one in Picture 1. Or they could spend the evening reading aloud and playing cards. Not all their amusements were peaceful ones, as Picture 2 shows!

Picture 1

Picture 2 This family are having fun in the living room, or 'parlour'. The Victorians often had very big families — how many children are in this one?

Can you see the piano in the corner? What else do you notice about the way the room is furnished?

There were special books of 'parlour games' or indoor amusements. The games and puzzles on this page all come from a book called *Indoor Amusements – card games and fireside fun*. (You can find the answers at the bottom of the page.)

PRISONERS' RELEASE PUZZLE

Take two pieces of string. Tie them round the wrists of two people as shown in the picture. The puzzle is for them to free themselves – or for anyone else to do it without untying the string.

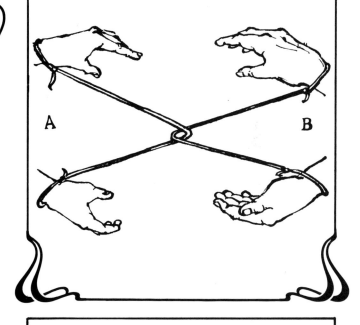

THE RULE OF CONTRARY

(*This is a game that a whole group could play*)
All stand around holding a tablecloth with one hand. One person acts as the leader. The leader holds the cloth with the left hand. With the right hand the leader makes pretend magic signs on the cloth, saying the words "Here we go round by the rule of contrary. When I say 'Hold fast' you must let go. When I say 'Let go' you must hold fast. Then either saying 'Let go' or 'Hold fast' the others must do exactly contrary (opposite) to what they are told. Anyone who should fail to do so must pay a forfeit."

FORFEITS

1 *Put your left hand where the right cannot touch it.*
2 *Leave the room with two legs and return with six.*
3 *Sit upon the fire.*
4 *Kiss a book inside and outside without opening it.*
5 *Put yourself through the keyhole.*

A RIDDLE

I am the child of the night and the child of the day. I have walked many a mile, but no-one has ever heard my footsteps. I have hands and feet, head and shoulders but no body. Although I have no eyes, I could not live without light. Tell me my name?

ANSWERS

Prisoners' release puzzle
B makes a loop to the string to pass under A's string, slips it over A's hands and both will be free.

Forfeits
1 Hold your right elbow with your left hand.
2 Go out of the room and come back with a chair.
3 Write the words 'the fire' on a piece of paper and sit on it.
4 Kiss the book inside the room, then go outside and kiss it.
5 Write 'yourself' on a piece of paper and push it through the keyhole.

Riddle
A man's shadow.

16 AN EVENING OUT

Picture 1 The Egyptian Hall was a popular London music hall.

As well as making their own entertainment indoors (see pages 32-33) many Victorian people enjoyed an evening out. One of the most popular places to go was the Music Hall (see Picture 1). Here, people could watch acrobats (like the ones in Picture 2), magicians, singers, comedians and many more.

People crowd these places to sit at a little table with a bottle of beer on it. (They keep) one eye on the acrobat, the other on the drink. A cigar hangs from the mouth. The ears listen to an Italian tune or a comic song.

One famous Victorian comedian was called Little Tich. He was only 4'6" tall! A member of the audience describes his act:

Strangest of all were his feet. These were put into enormous boots — long, narrow and flat. He throws his hat into the air and the little stick that he carries. He tries to decide which to pick up. As he bends to pick up his hat, the toe of his big boot pushes the hat out of reach. Sometimes it only goes a little way, sometimes it jumps like a frog. Then suddenly Tich kicks or hits it in such a way that it spins into the air and he catches it on his head. The band starts again.

Picture 2

Not everyone was as popular as Little Tich. Audiences soon let performers know if they did not like them. This is what would happen:

In a minute you notice that people begin to talk. They flutter their programmes. They might hum a tune. Then you hear laughter. A few yells come from the gallery. A general uproar and shouts. 'Take me back to mother', 'Shut up, chuck him out', 'Shut up I can see yer Christmas dinner'. The band plays louder as a large number in the audience get to their feet. The curtains comes down. That is called getting the bird!

Usually the audiences enjoyed their night out. It gave them a chance to laugh and join in popular songs like this one:

Champagne Charlie is my name!
Champagne Charlie is my name!
Good for any game at night boys!
So, who'll come out and join me in a spree?

✯✯✯ TO DO ✯✯✯

1. a) How do you think the Music Hall got its name? **b)** List three acts that people could go to see. **c)** What was 'getting the bird'?

2. Look carefully at Picture 1. In it there is a clue about what happened to many Music Halls. Can you guess what they were turned into?

17 'IT CANNOT DIE'

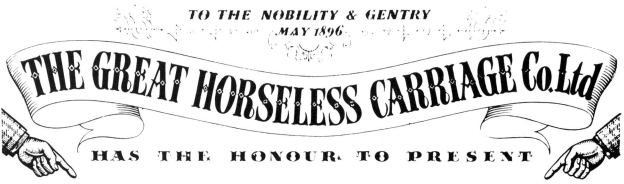

Picture 1

On 12 February 1898 Henry Lindfield climbed into his new car. His son Bernard got in too. They set off for Brighton. Bernard later described what happened:

As we went down Purley Hill my bag suddenly fell out. My father tried to stop the car. It went from side to side out of control. It then turned right round. It ran through a wire fence and hit an iron post. It then turned over against a tree.

Bernard was thrown clear. His father died later. He was the first car driver to be killed in an accident in Britain.

The motor car was a new invention at that time. Here is a description of one of these early cars:

A little open thing. Moving along on rubber covered wheels. A panting noise comes from the square-shaped box in the front. Two, and sometimes three people are seated in it. One drives using a handle. To see it race past at 20 miles an hour takes the breath away.

Early cars were very expensive. Car makers used advertisements like the one in Picture 1 to get people to buy them. They tried hard to show how much better a car was than a horse-drawn carriage.

Here are some of the reasons given in another advertisement:

1 It needs no stable...
2 It needs no grooming...
3 There is no manure heap to poison the air.
4 It cannot kick or run away.
5 It is under control more than a horse.
6 It costs nothing to keep and doesn't eat its head off.
7 It cannot die or fall sick.
8 It will do more work than two horses and travel twice as fast.
9 It can be stopped safely and in half the distance.
10 It isn't cruel to make it go up steep hills or go fast.

Cars got faster and faster. The police set 'traps' to try and stop speeding. Here are some notes from a doctor's diary:

2 Sept 1902 Over 70 miles in the car without anything going wrong.

✯✯✯ TO DO ✯✯✯

1. Can you think of ten reasons why the horse-drawn carriage might be better than a motor car?

2. Write a description of a modern car to be read by someone who has never seen one.

---

23 Sept 1902 The motor behaved very well. Lit my new car lamp for the first time — very good. Came home sometimes at 60 miles an hour, never under 40. Speed very fast, bumping uncomfortable and the dust awful. The A.A. lookouts always saved us from police speed traps.

This chapter started with a road accident. Unfortunately there were many more. Picture 2 shows a crash at a cross-road. It was taken in 1914.

Picture 2

18 BESIDE THE SEASIDE

Have you ever been to the seaside? Perhaps you visited Blackpool, Bournemouth or Brighton? These towns, and many others like them, became famous holiday resorts in Victorian times.

Sea-bathing first became popular in the eighteenth century. But it was not meant to be enjoyed. People thought that sea water was good for them. A Dr Alexander explained:

A bather should crouch down in the water until his whole body is covered. Then he should get out and dry off. . . He should then walk slowly home and have some hot soup or tea. . .

Bathers were taken out to the water in little huts on wheels called *bathing machines*. You can see some of them in Picture 1. Queen Victoria went for her first sea bathe on 30 July 1847. She wrote in her diary:

Drove down to the beach with my maid and went into the bathing machine where I undressed and bathed in the sea. . . a very nice bathing woman attending me. I thought it delightful until I put my head under the water. . .

The spread of the railways (see pages 16-17) meant that many more people could afford to travel to the seaside. The London to Brighton railway opened in

Picture 1

1841. Soon people could go on cheap day excursions to the seaside.

Another popular seaside town was Margate. Londoners could travel there by boat up the Thames. They came home late at night, tired but happy:

We had a very pleasant trip home from Margate and everybody was happy. A passenger who had more to drink than eat got into a coil of cable on the boat home and fell asleep. . . like a bird in its nest; another took off his boots and fell asleep in his socks.

As well as holidaymakers the beaches were crowded with people offering entertainment, or selling food, drink and souvenirs (see Picture 2). This is what it was like at Yarmouth:

Take a seat and your troubles begin. 'Here's your chocolate creams, buns two a penny. Yarmouth rock, a penny a bar, apples, penny a bag, lemonade threepence a bottle, milk penny a glass'. (There was) so much street music that we would have spent all our money if we had paid them one penny each — some play the accordion. One man with an organ was so loud that we couldn't stand it.

The seaside towns grew quickly to cope with all the visitors. Hotels and boarding houses sprang up along the sea fronts. Some of them were very grand, but others were not so good, as this music hall song suggests:

I am a bug, a seaside bug,
When folks in bed are lying snug,
About their skin we walk and creep,
and feast upon them while they sleep.

Picture 2 This little girl is selling shell-covered souvenirs on the beach. The word *souvenir* is French for 'to remember'. Visitors liked to take home something to remind them of their holiday.

✯✯✯ TO DO ✯✯✯

1. Make a list of everything you can see happening in Picture 1. Which things in the picture would you *not* expect to see at the seaside today?

2. Imagine you are the little girl selling souvenirs in Picture 2. Write a story about your day at the seaside: collecting shells, selling your souvenirs to well-off holiday-makers, making the boxes and ornaments to sell.

19 'THIS WONDERFUL PLACE'

Have you always lived in your town? Perhaps you moved there from another part of the country? How did you feel? Were you excited, or sad?

The people in Picture 1 are leaving Britain for ever. Thousands of people *emigrated* (went to live abroad) in Victorian times. Why did they go? This letter may help you understand. It was printed in the *Bradford Observer* newspaper in December 1848:

Picture 1 Emigrants about to set sail for Canada.

Now father, I think Australia is wonderful. Work is well paid here. We have a beautiful cottage in a gentleman's garden. Wood to burn, water and vegetables. We call it paradise. We have melons, peaches, oranges, grapes and tobacco. Flour, lamb, beef and tea are very cheap. I often think of my poor father and mother and brothers and sisters. They were often close to death from hunger. We have plenty here of everything and some to spare. We often talk about the poor slaves of England. I hope that you will let the gentlemen read this letter that gave me the money. They got me to this wonderful place.

The person who wrote that letter was lucky. Life was not always so good for the emigrants. The journey by sea to the new country usually took many weeks. There were strict rules on board ship. These are just a few of them:

1 The passengers when dressed (are) to roll up their beds, to sweep the decks including the space under the bottom of the berths and throw the dirt overboard before breakfast.
2 Passengers must take it in turns to clean the ladders, sweep the decks after every meal and scrape them after breakfast.
3 Passengers to be in bed by 10 pm.

Picture 2 Most emigrants faced a lot of hard work when they arrived in a new country. Often they had to build their own homes, and clear a patch of land to grow food.

When they got off the boat many emigrants had to face another long journey. Mrs Jameson went to Canada. She described her long journey inland:

The lines of trees seemed to go on for ever. The forests are deep. No white man has ever been into them. There are long silences. Then a bird sings or a giant bullfrog splashes into the water. The wagon we were on often sank into deep holes. Sometimes we saw a smashed wheel or a broken cart. The journey was very rough. I had to hang on to the wagon rail. By the time we arrived my arms ached and my hands were blistered.

When the journey ended the settlers had to face even more hard work. Many had to build themselves a house and grow their own food (see Picture 2). But in spite of the hard work most emigrants were not sorry that they had come. They looked forward to their new lives.

✯✯✯ TO DO ✯✯✯

1. a) Why did the young man who wrote to the Bradford Observer think Australia was wonderful? **b)** What did he say about life in England? **c)** How could he afford to go to Australia?

2. What dangers faced Mrs Jameson on her journey inland?

3. Imagine you are one of the emigrants going to Canada in Picture 1. Write about your thoughts as you wait to go on board ship. Are you sorry to be leaving England or looking forward to your new life? Are you frightened of the voyage? Will you miss the friends and family left behind?

20 THE BRITISH IN INDIA

In Victorian times Britain had a huge Empire which stretched all over the world (see Picture 1). Queen Victoria was ruler of all the countries in the Empire. One of the most important was India. Picture 2 shows a splendid throne sent to Queen Victoria from India.

A man called John Beames spent 25 years in India as a government official. Later he wrote a book about his time there. This is what he said about the rainy season:

It (the rain) begins before daybreak on the first of the month, and when you go to bed on the 31st it is still drizzling on. . . Your boots grow a crop of mould every night. My books are losing their bindings and curling up into limp masses of pulp.

In the summer the temperature soared

Picture 2   This throne was given to Queen Victoria by the people of India. It was put on show at the Great Exhibition.

Picture 1   In Victorian times the British Empire was at its greatest. This map shows Britain's *colonies* (countries ruled by Britain) in 1900. Find out from an atlas what these countries are called today.

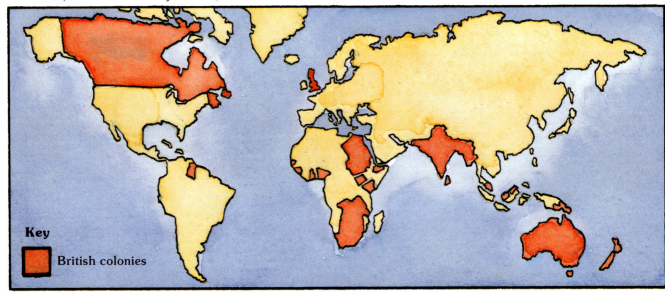

Key
British colonies

and there were weeks of blazing sunshine. There were poisonous insects too. Minnie Wood went to India with her husband, who was a British soldier. They were warned "*Be sure to shake boots or shoes before putting them on. There might be scorpions, centipedes and other insects inside.*"

Even so, Minnie liked her new life. She wrote:

The houses are very quiet. The Indian servants never wear shoes. One servant is used to pull a fan backwards and forwards all the time. Last night we slept under a mosquito net in a huge room. There are bath and dressing rooms added to each bedroom. It is all wonderful.

Picture 3 shows a British woman with her Indian servants. The British lived well, but most of the people they ruled were very poor. Millions died from hunger and disease. After a visit to Calcutta Minnie Wood wrote "*I do not like Calcutta at all. It is common to see men begging. Little children run along beside our carriage begging for money.*"

John Beames tried to deal with the problems he found in one town:

Everywhere one came upon pools of black, stagnant water covered with weed. . . the walls of houses and huts were green with mould, every hedge and thicket were used as a latrine (toilet). . . We did what we could by setting up a staff of sweepers to remove refuse (rubbish) and filth, cutting down the jungle, and fining people for not keeping their premises clean. Drains were made, roads and bridges mended. . .

But many of the British kept themselves apart from the Indian people, as this writer discovered:

I asked one lady what she had seen of the country and the natives. . . 'Oh nothing!' said she: 'thank goodness, I know nothing about them, nor I don't wish to: really I think the less one sees and knows of them the better!'

Picture 3

✯✯✯ TO DO ✯✯✯

1. a) What happened to John Beames' books? **b)** Why was Minnie warned to shake her shoes?

2. a) Why was one of Minnie's servants used to pull a fan? **b)** What was the mosquito net for?

3. How did John Beames set about changing things in one town?

21 HOW TO BE AN EXPLORER

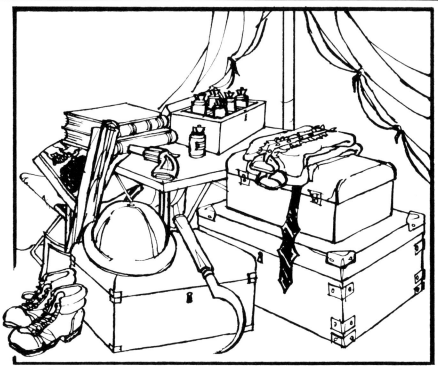

Picture 1 Major Thompson went to Africa in 1883. He wrote a list of things he thought an explorer should take:
Take eight watertight boxes for clothes and books. Take four suits and six shirts and three pairs of boots. Don't take heavy boots as they make the feet scalding hot . . . Take a roomy tent and blankets. Also a folding table and chair. Of course a medicine chest, but also a revolver, axes and cutting hooks.

In Victorian times many people in America and Europe wanted to find out more about far-off places. Who lived there? What plants grew there? What new animals might they find?

A lot of British explorers went to Africa. These *expeditions* (journeys) were difficult and often dangerous. Explorers needed a lot of special equipment. Picture 1 shows what the inside of an explorer's tent might have looked like. A traveller called Francis Galton did not like tents because *"in a tent a man sleeps well. He hears and sees nothing. Enemies may creep up and spear him."*

The same writer gave this advice to explorers:

The natives will usually run away in fright when you get to a village. If you need for anything just walk into their huts. You take what you want and leave proper payment.

One of the biggest problems was finding fresh drinking water. Francis Galton watched what the African people did:

In Africa the natives carry a little fat or butter. When they are thirsty they eat a little. This stops the person wanting water.

Dr David Livingstone was a famous Victorian explorer. On one of his expeditions in Africa he got lost. An American called Henry Morton Stanley set out to find him. Picture 2 is a drawing of one of his camps. Stanley did find Livingstone. When they got back to Britain they were welcomed as heroes.

But the Africans did not feel the same way about them. When the African King Mojimba took his tribe to meet Stanley:

. . . we prepared a feast and dressed up. We got the canoes ready. We were all singing and dancing. We moved towards his boats. As we got near – 'Bang, bang!'. We were frightened. Many fell silent. They were dead. Blood came from little holes in their bodies. We sped back to our village. That was the worst enemy our country had ever seen.

Other explorers got on well with the African people. One was an English woman called Mary Kingsley. She lived for a while with a tribe called the Fans.

> ★ ★ ★ **TO DO** ★ ★ ★
>
> **1.** Draw two columns. In one list all the things Major Thompson said an explorer needed. In the other column put down why you think he suggested taking each thing.
>
> **2.** Why did Francis Galton disagree with Major Thompson?
>
> **3.** Look at Picture 2. Make a list of everything you can see happening in the picture.

She wrote

We soon had a kind of friendship. We knew that we were all human beings. We knew that it was better to drink together than fight. We could have killed each other but we made sure that this did not happen.

Picture 2 This drawing was made by Henry Morton Stanley while he was on his way to find Dr Livingstone, in Africa.

22 THE NEW CENTURY

The Twentieth Century began on 1 January 1901. This is how the *Daily Mail* newspaper announced its start:

The hand of the clock has reached the quarter, and is pressing on to midnight... the hand steals on... the nineteenth century is gasping out its breath — Boom!
The first stroke of midnight crashes through the frosty air and is hailed by a roar of jubilation. The succeeding strokes are almost unheard; they are all lost and drowned in the tumult of cheering. Hurrah! The twentieth century has dawned.

Many people tried to guess what life would be like in the new century. Pictures 1-3 show some of their ideas. How many of them were right?

Sir Aston Webb was a famous architect. He wrote a book describing what he thought London would be like in the future. In it, he pretended that he could travel forward in time:

I asked why everything looked so bright and clean... it was because they had done away with the smoke and only used smokeless fuels now. I noticed that besides the railway tracks there were great roads stretching out in all ways. They were 40 metres wide. There were two divisions — one for slow and one for fast traffic. Tramways had gone. People had wireless telephones and wireless electric lights. There was a belt of green round London.

In 1898 a young journalist called Arthur Mee described an invention of the future — the Pleasure Telephone. Can you work out what he meant?

Patti and Paderewski (famous musicians) may yet entertain us in our own drawing-rooms... Who knows but that in time we may sit in our armchairs listening to

Picture 1

Picture 2

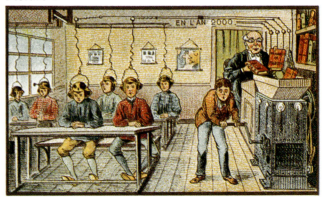

Picture 3 This is one Victorian artist's idea of what an air and sea battle might look like in the year 2000. Look carefully at the picture. How many of his ideas have already come true?

the speeches of Her Majesty's Ministers (MPs)... It will be so entertaining and useful that it will make life happier all round... It will make millions merry who have never been merry before...

But not everyone thought that everything in the future would be better. In 1908, in a book called *The War in the Air* the novelist H G Wells wrote: "*No place is safe. No place is at peace. The war comes through the air. Bombs drop in the night.*" Six years later the First World War began.

The celebrations for the New Year were soon cut short. On 22 January 1901 Queen Victoria died. All over Britain people mourned, and hundreds came to watch her funeral procession in London:

We saw the procession descend the hill... and wind slowly up the opposite slope, till the figures were lost in the haze and the trees... It was a wonderful afternoon, and I shall never cease to be glad that I saw it and was one of the few who saw her carried from her home to be laid to rest.

The Victorian Age had ended, just as the new century began.

✯✯✯ TO DO ✯✯✯

1. Make a list of all the *predictions* (guesses about the future) you can find on these pages. How many of them have come true?

2. When will the Twenty-first century begin? What will life be like then? Make up some predictions of your own about the next 100 years. Draw pictures of some of your ideas.

47

HOW TO BE A HISTORIAN

First of all, get yourself a pocket notebook. Take it with you when you visit museums, historical places and libraries. Jot down important information on the Victorians in it, and draw anything that looks interesting.

You will then need a big scrapbook or exercise book. When you get home from each visit, start a new page, put the date at the top, and write down carefully everything you saw and did. Look at the notes in your notebook to remind yourself. You could copy some of your drawings into the book.

Historians need to keep a 'record' or diary like this. It stops them from forgetting things; and it is useful to have all their information in one place. Write on the cover of your scrapbook

The Victorians
A Record kept by (your name)

Here are some ways of finding information to put in your Record:

VISITING MUSEUMS
Always remember to
- decide what you want to look for in the museum before you visit it. For example, you might want to look at Victorian toys or furniture. Usually there are so many things in museums that it is impossible to look at *everything* properly.
- check if there are any leaflets or museum guides on sale. These will help you to find your way around and explain some of the things on show.
- check if you can find any postcards of the things on show. They would be useful to stick in your Record.

If you can, try to visit the Victoria and Albert Museum in London. It was named after Queen Victoria and Prince Albert, and it has a good collection of Victorian things.

VISITING HISTORICAL PLACES
(like Osborne House, the Albert Memorial and other places you have read about in this book) Always remember to

- go first to the shop where they sell leaflets and guides. You will probably be able to buy postcards and maps for your Record there too.

- try hard to imagine what the place *used* to look like. In your notebook, do a drawing of how it looks today; then do another one, showing how you think it looked in Victorian times. Put people and animals in this second drawing.

WATCHING, LISTENING AND READING
People are always discovering new things about the Victorians. Watch out for television and radio programmes about these discoveries. You can find out more about them in newspapers, which you can read in public libraries. Libraries also have lots of books on Victorians. Here is a list of some good ones to look out for:

Growing Up During the Industrial Revolution, Penny Clarke, Batsford
Growing Up in Victorian Britain, Sheila Ferguson, Batsford
They Saw It Happen 1689-1897, T. Charles-Edwards and B. Richardson, Blackwell
The History of Everyday Things in England (Vols 3, 4) M. and C. Quennell, Batsford

Remember to write down in your Record all the new things that you learn from these books.